# Bible Memory Activity Book

## Mary Currier

**Baker Books**

A Division of Baker Book House Co
Grand Rapids, Michigan 49516

©1994 by Mary Currier

Published by Baker Books
a division of Baker Book House Company
P.O. Box 6287, Grand Rapids, MI 49516-6287

ISBN 0-8010-2578-8

Printed in the United States of America

# 1. The Books of the Old Testament Tell . . .

ABOUT GOD IN HEAVEN

Fill in the spaces in the "books" below using the letters in the matching shapes above.

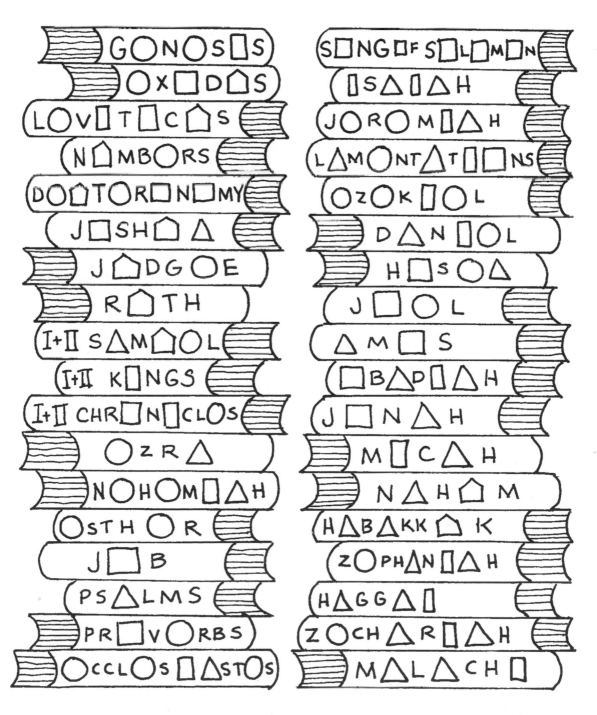

# 2. Genesis 1:1

Find Genesis 1:1 in your Bible. Then fill in the blanks below to finish the verse. The pictures under the lines will help you.

In the beginning God created the

_____

and the

_____ .

# 3. Genesis 1:27

Add the math problems in the figure. Match the answer to the number under the lines. Put the word from the math problem on the lines.

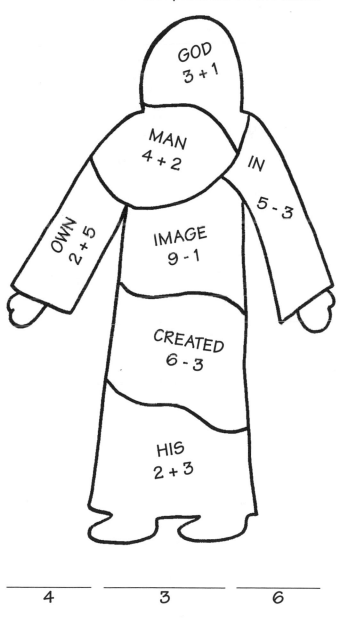

GOD
3 + 1

MAN
4 + 2

IN
5 - 3

OWN
2 + 5

IMAGE
9 - 1

CREATED
6 - 3

HIS
2 + 3

___ ___ ___
 4   3   6

___ ___ ___ ___.
 2   5   7   8    Genesis 1:27

# 4. Genesis 2:7

Fill in the puzzle with words from Genesis 2:7 using the clues at the bottom of the page.

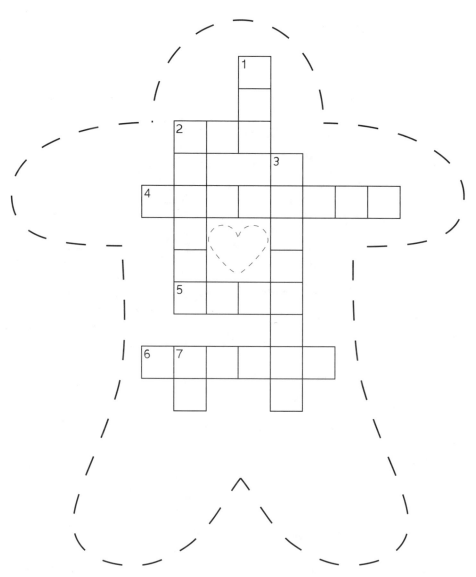

**Down**

1. _____ man became a living being
2. of the _____ and breathed
3. and _____ into his nostrils
7. dust _____ the ground

**Across**

2. _____ formed the man
4. into his _____ the breath of life
5. the _____ of the ground
6. God _____ the man

# 5. Genesis 18:14

Follow the words from Genesis 18:14 through the puzzle.

IS ANYTHING TOO HARD FOR THE LORD?

Start

| I | S | A | N | O | G | F |
|---|---|---|---|---|---|---|
| O | R | N | T | H | E | L |
| O | T | Y | O | O | H | A |
| R | H | D | T | I | S | R |
| A | I | N | G | N | F | D |
| Y | T | H | T | R | O | I |
| N | G | T | H | O | O | H |
| A | R | D | E | F | O | R |
| T | H | E | L | O | R | D |

Finish

# 6. Exodus 20:12

God gave Moses ten commandments to help people live right. The fifth commandment states that we should honor our

F ___ ___ H ___ R  and  ___ O T ___ ___ R.

(Fill in the missing letters.)

To honor means to show respect and give much care and consideration to someone. Do you honor your parents?

Draw a picture of your parents.

# 7. Deuteronomy 31:13

1. Color the project below with colored pencils.
2. Cut out on the outer lines.
3. Fold on lines to form a pocket shape.
4. Apply glue on tab and fasten to hold.
5. When dry, use as a bookmark by putting on the corner of pages you are marking in a book.

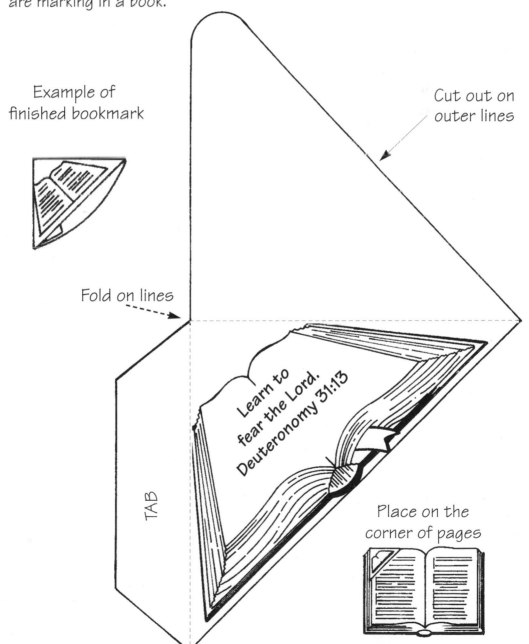

Example of finished bookmark

Cut out on outer lines

Fold on lines

TAB

Learn to fear the Lord. Deuteronomy 31:13

Place on the corner of pages

# 8. Joshua 1:8

Read Joshua 1:8, then complete the sentences using words from the word box.

1. Joshua 1:8 is telling about the Book of the _____ .

2. The Book of the Law should not depart from your _____ .

3. To think about something a lot is to _____ .

4. You should meditate on the Book of the Law _____

   and _____ .

5. Do everything that is _____ in the Book of the Law.

6. Joshua 1:8 says you will be _____ if you obey.

## ⁓◌⊃ Word Box ◌⊃⌒

Law

day

meditate

night

mouth

written

prosperous

# 9. Joshua 23:11

Unscramble the words below and put the word on the line above it. Then print Joshua 23:11 in the heart shape below.

_____          _____          _____
        VOEL                      HTE                      DRLO

_____          _____.
        RUOY                      OGD              Joshua 23:11

# 10. Joshua 24:15

Look up Joshua 24:15 in your Bible. Fill in the blanks in the house using the puzzle pieces at the bottom of the page. (There will be two puzzle pieces you will not use.)

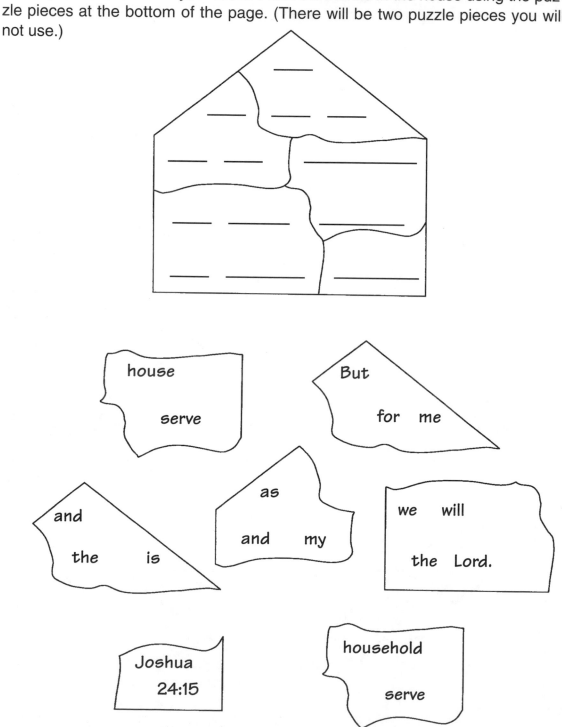

house

serve

But

for   me

and

the     is

as

and     my

we     will

the   Lord.

Joshua

24:15

household

serve

# 11. 1 Samuel 12:20

Color the chart and cut it out. Hang it on your refrigerator. Mark the days as you do the chores.

 My Chore Chart

| Name of Chore | ★ Sun | ✿ Mon | ❀ Tue | ♥ Wed | ❀ Thur | ✿ Fri | ★ Sat |
|---|---|---|---|---|---|---|---|
| Take out garbage | | | | | | | |
| Put away toys | | | | | | | |
| Set the table | | | | | | | |
| | | | | | | | |

Serve the Lord with all your heart.

1 Samuel 12:20

# 12. 1 Samuel 16:7

Read 1 Samuel 16:7 in your Bible. Fill in the blanks using the pictures for clues.

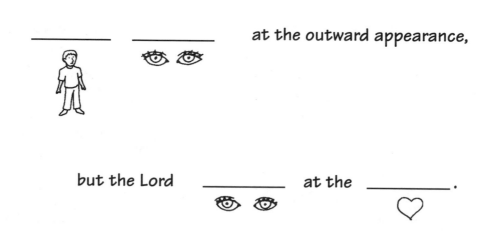

_____ _____ at the outward appearance,

but the Lord _____ at the _____.

Match the words to the correct picture.

**What does man look at?**

**What does God look at?**

# 13. 2 Chronicles 20:15

Use the vowels in the small stones at the bottom of the page to fill in the blanks.

F __ R        TH __
  1             5

B __ TTL __         __ S
  3      5           2

N __ T        Y __ __ RS,
  1            1   4

B __ T        G __ D'S.  2 Chronicles
  4            1                20:15

# 14. Job 29:3

Look up the Bible references below. Find the color in that verse and match it with the number to color the picture.

1.  Matthew 16:2

2.  Mark 15:17

3.  Exodus 26:4

4.  Revelation 19:14

5.  Leviticus 13:32

6.  1 Kings 18:45

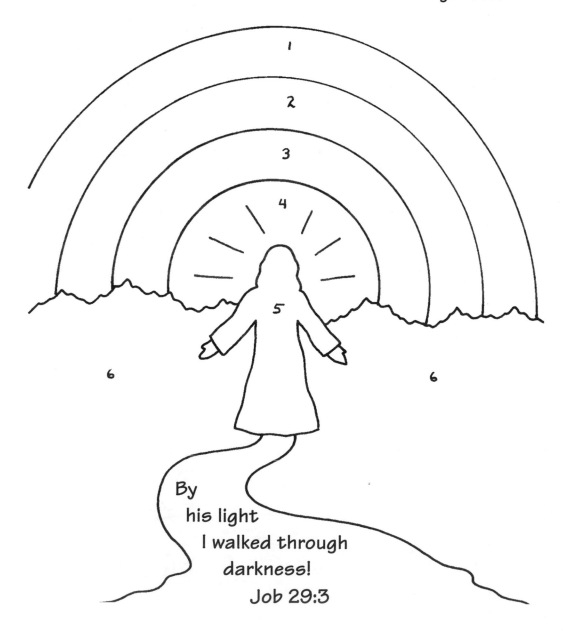

By
his light
I walked through
darkness!
Job 29:3

# 15. Psalm 1

Fill in the missing words from verses in Psalm 1. Then unscramble the letters from the boxes to fill in the blanks at the bottom of this page.

Blessed is __ __ □ man who does not walk in the counsel

__ __ the wicked (verse 1).

But his delight is in the __ __ __ of the __ __ □ __,

and on his law he meditates day and __ __ __ __ __ (verse 2).

He is like a tree __ __ __ __ __□__ by streams of water (verse 3).

Therefore the wicked will not

__ __ __□__ in the

judgment, __ __ __ sinners

in the assembly of the

__ __ __ __ __ __ __ __ __(verse 5).

**A righteous person is like a**

__ __ __ __.

# 16. Psalm 2:11

Follow the maze. Put the letters on the lines at the bottom of the page.

**start**

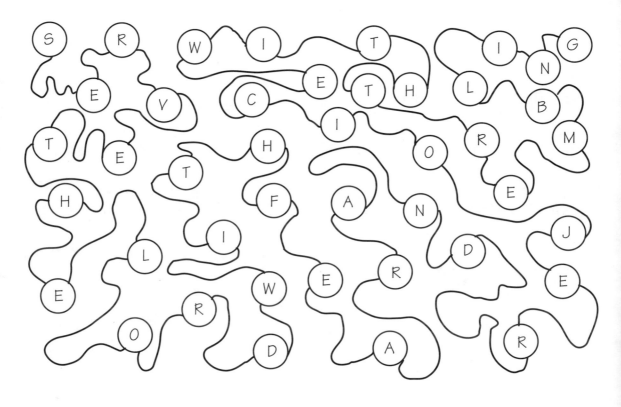

_____

_____

_____

# 17. Psalm 7:17

Start at the * in the border. Print every other letter on the lines in the oval.

Psalm 7:17

# 18. Psalm 17:8

Read Psalm 17:8 in your Bible. Then circle the correct words to the verse.

Keep me/you as the orange/apple of your/the eye; hide/find me in/under the feather/shadow of thy/your wings.

Psalm 17:8

# 19. Psalm 23:1

Cut ✂

1. Color the project below and cut out on outer lines.

2. Fold on the dotted lines.

3. Apply glue on tab.

4. Fold together to make a stand-up plaque as shown below.

5. Set up as a reminder that the Lord is your guide.

**Example of finished project**

The **LORD** is my **SHEPHERD**

Psalm 23:1

glue a cotton ball here

Apply glue here.

# 20. Psalm 24:8

Color all the areas below that do not have words from Psalm 24:8.

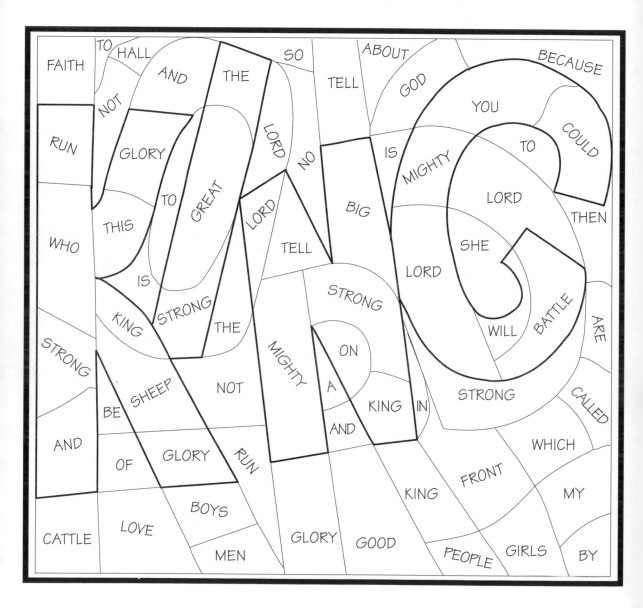

**What word do you have left?** _____

# 21. Psalm 25:4

Read Psalm 25:4. Fill in the blanks.

_____ me _____

_____, O Lord,

_____ me _____

_____.

Psalm 25:4

# 22. Psalm 27:1

Use the words from Psalm 27:1 to do the dot-to-dot.

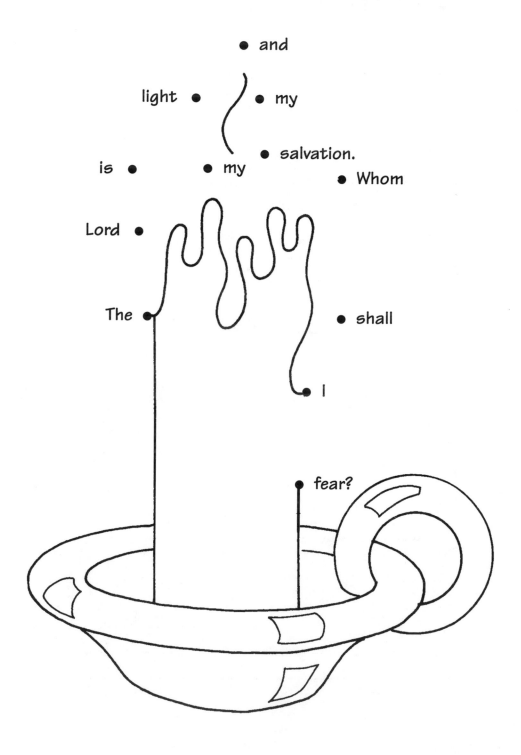

# 23. Psalm 33:4

Color the project below. Cut out on heavy lines. Fold on dotted line. To help you learn this important verse, put it on your dresser, where you will often see it.

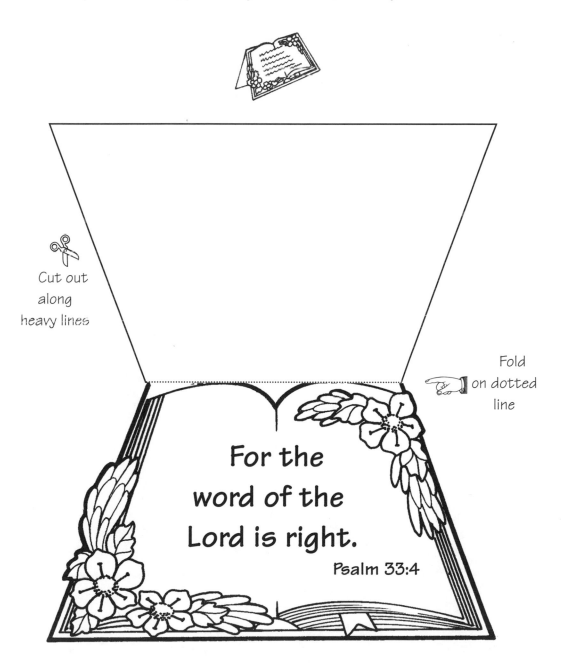

Cut out
along
heavy lines

Fold
on dotted
line

For the
word of the
Lord is right.

Psalm 33:4

# 24. Psalm 33:12

Put the words in the stars in the correct order on the lines.

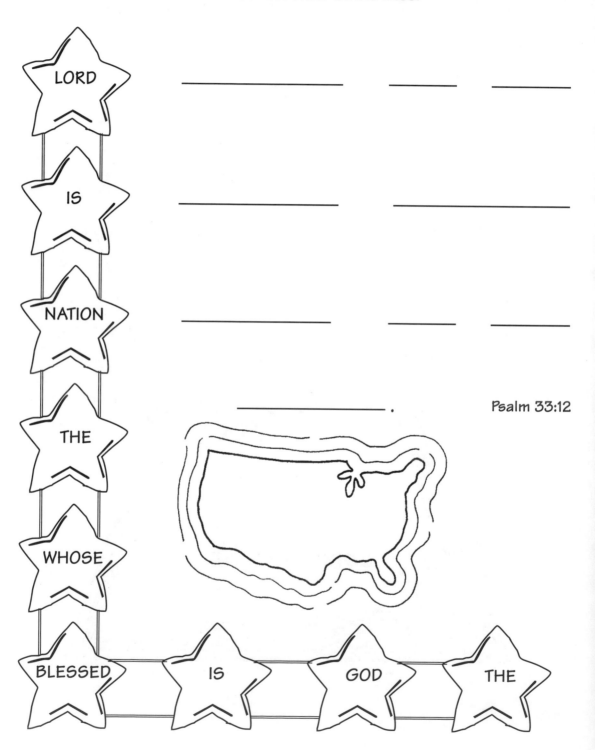

_____ _____ _____

_____ _____

_____ _____

_____ .          Psalm 33:12

LORD

IS

NATION

THE

WHOSE

BLESSED   IS   GOD   THE

# 25. Psalm 34:8

Use the letters in the fruit border to fill in the blanks.

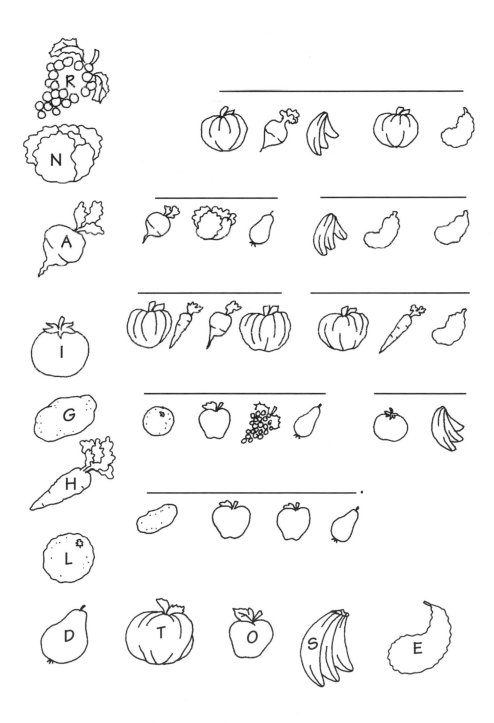

# 26. Psalm 34:15

Work the crossword puzzle using the clues below.

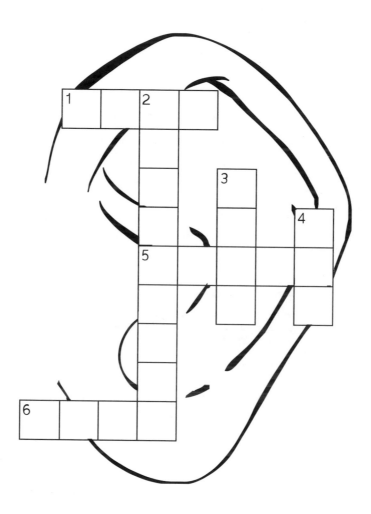

## Across

1. The fifth word in Psalm 34:15
5. The word before "cry" in Psalm 34:15
6. The word after "his" in Psalm 34:15

## Down

2. The longest word in the first half of Psalm 34:15
3. You can see with these
4. The last word in Psalm 34:15

# 27. Psalm 37:1–8

Use the clues at the bottom of the page to fill in the blanks.

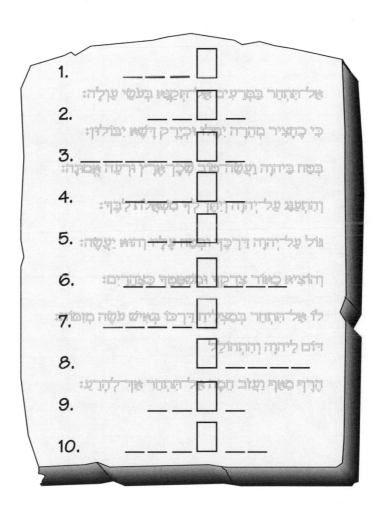

1. This word is in verse 1 of Psalm 37 and starts with the letter "F."
2. "Trust in the _____" is in verse 3.
3. Verse 1 says we should not be _____.
4. You can walk on this and the word is in verse 2.
5. The second word in verse 1 is _____.
6. The first word in verse 4 is _____.

7. This is a color and it is mentioned in verse 2.
8. In verse 4, God promises to give us the desires of our _____.
9. "_____ patiently for him" is in verse 7.
10. The first word in verse 5 is _____.

# 28. Psalm 37:27

Color in the areas with dots to find a hidden message.

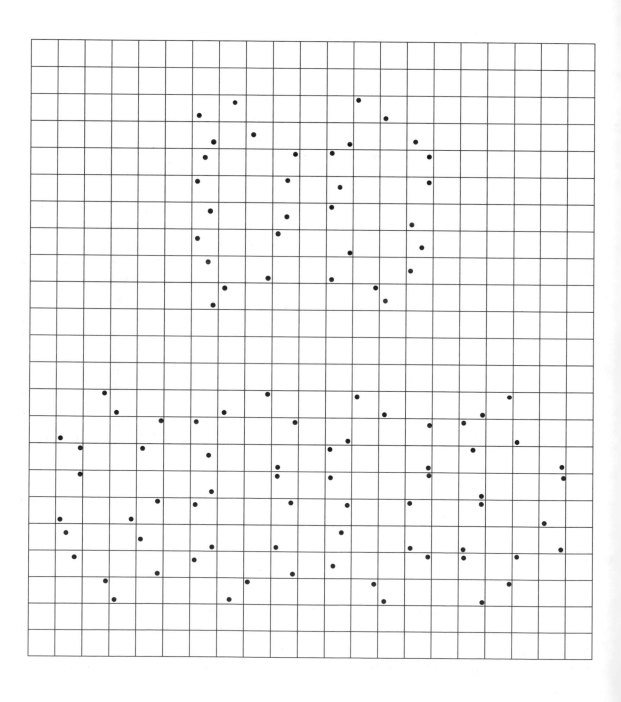

# 29. Psalm 42:1

Read this verse, then circle the correct answer to each question.

## What kind of animal is mentioned in this verse?

goat
dove
pig
cow
hart
chicken
sheep
lion
deer

## What did the animal want?

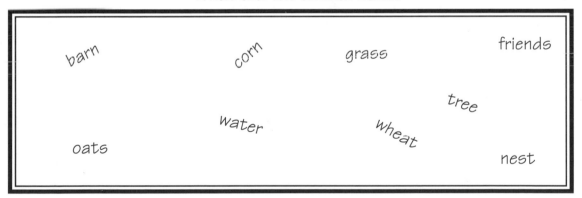

barn
corn
grass
friends
tree
water
wheat
oats
nest

## According to this verse what should we want?

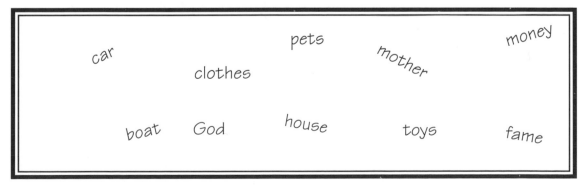

car
pets
mother
money
clothes
boat
God
house
toys
fame

# 30. Psalm 46:1

Trace over the letters and color the picture.

God is our refuge and strength

# 31. Psalm 46:10

Use the Braille code to fill in the blanks.

___ ___ ___ ___ ___ ___ ___, ___ ___ ___ ___ ___ ___ ___

___ ___ ___ ___ ___ ___ ___ ___ ___ ___ . Psalm 46:10

| A | B | C | D | E | F | G | H | I | J | K |
|---|---|---|---|---|---|---|---|---|---|---|

| L | M | N | O | P | Q | R | S | T | U | V |
|---|---|---|---|---|---|---|---|---|---|---|

| W | X | Y | Z |
|---|---|---|---|

# 32. Psalm 48:1

Color the project and cut it out.

1. Apply glue where shown.

2. Match to form a ring.

back side

3. Set project up.

finished project

Apply Glue Here

Great is the Lord
Psalm 48:1

Cut along heavy line

# 33. Psalm 51:2

Use letters from the raindrops to fill in the blanks.

__ __ __ __ __ __ __    __ __
3  7  1  8  11  6  1    10  1

__ __ __ __    __ __
4  5  9  10    10  2

__ __ __ . Psalm 51:2
6  12  11

What does God say he will do if you pray and call on him?
Fill in the blanks using the code at the bottom of the page.

I will __ __ __ __ __ __ him.
     1 8 11 15 4 10

I will __ __   __ __ __ __ him
    2 4   15 6 12 5

__ __   __ __ __ __ __ __ __.
6 8   12 10 9 13 2 7 4

I will __ __ __ __ __ __ __ him
    3 4 7 6 14 4 10

__ __ __   __ __ __ __ __ him.
1 8 3   5 9 8 9 10

| A | B | D | E | H | I | L | N | O | R | S | T | U | V | W |
|---|---|---|---|---|---|---|---|---|---|---|---|---|---|---|
| 1 | 2 | 3 | 4 | 5 | 6 | 7 | 8 | 9 | 10 | 11 | 12 | 13 | 14 | 15 |

# 35. Psalm 100

Answer the questions using verses from Psalm 100.

SERVE THE LORD WITH GLADNESS

Verse 1—Whom should we praise?

_____

Verse 2—We should serve the Lord with

_____

Verse 3—Who made us?

_____

Verse 4—We should enter into his gates with

_____

Verse 5—Who is good?

_____

FOR THE LORD IS GOOD

# 36. Psalm 102:1

Color the project below. Cut out on outer lines. Fold on dotted lines and glue tabs behind frame to make it 3-D.

Cut alon
heavy lir

glue here

glue here

Hear my prayer,

O Lord.

Psalm 102:1

glue here

glue here

# 37. Psalm 103:12

Read Psalm 103:12. Then circle the correct words to finish the verse.

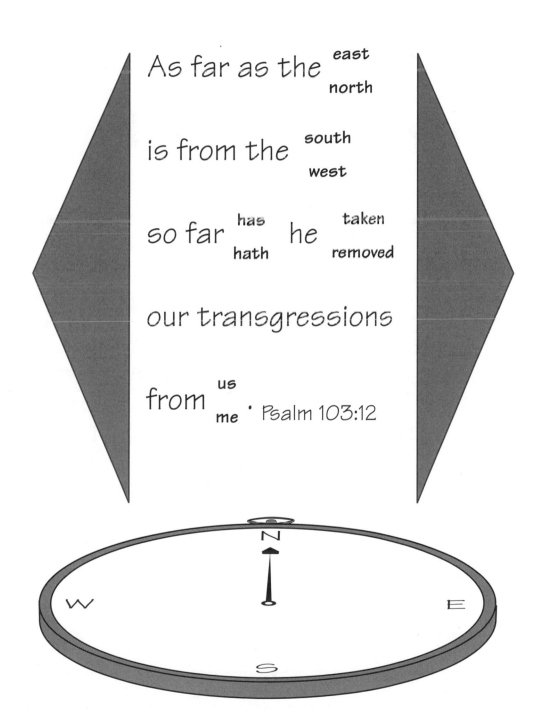

As far as the ^east / north

is from the ^south / west

so far ^has / hath he ^taken / removed

our transgressions

from ^us / me · Psalm 103:12

# 38. Psalm 111:10

Follow the words from Psalm 111:10 in the dot-to-dot.

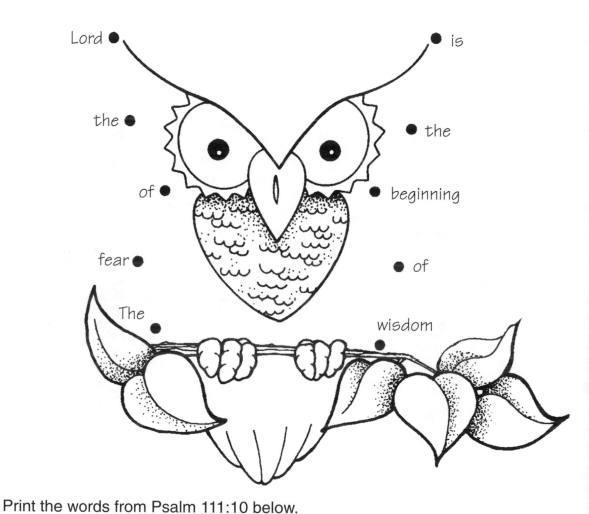

Lord ●                    ● is

the ●                    ● the

of ●                    ● beginning

fear ●                    ● of

The ●                    wisdom ●

Print the words from Psalm 111:10 below.

_____

_____

_____

_____

_____

# 39. Psalm 116:1

Color in the letters that have dots to find the words of Psalm 116:1.

# 40. Psalm 118:24

Who made this day?

Find the matching symbols in the picture above. Then write the first letter of the object on the lines.

# 41. Psalm 119:11

Where should you hide God's Word? Draw exactly what you see in the bottom squares into the same numbered square at the top of the page to find out.

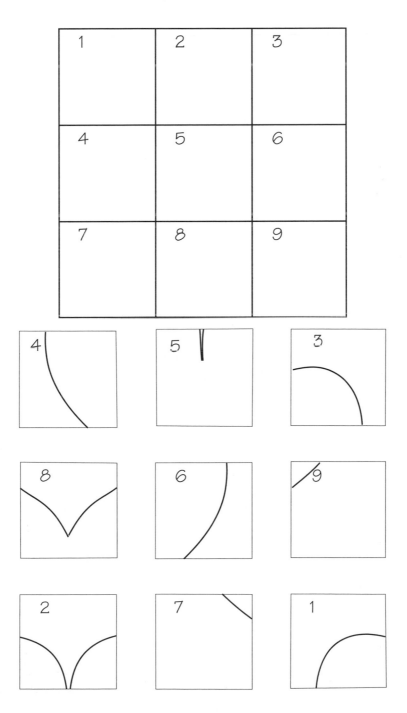

# 42. Psalm 122:1

Psalm 122:1 says to be happy to go into the house of the Lord.
Follow the dots to find out what the house of the Lord is.

# 43. Psalm 139:23

Print every other letter on the lines below. Begin at "start."

\_ \_ \_ \_ \_ \_ \_ \_ \_ \_ , \_ \_ \_ \_ \_ , \_ \_ \_ \_ \_ \_ \_ \_ \_

\_ \_ \_ \_ \_ \_ \_ \_ . Psalm 139:23

start

# 44. Psalm 145:9

Color by number.

1 = yellow
2 = red
3 = blue

# 45. Proverbs 3:5

Make a postcard to send to a friend.

1. Color and cut out the project below.
2. Glue it to one side of a 4" X 6" card.
3. Use the other side of the card for the address.

# 46. Proverbs 6:6

Learn Proverbs 6:6. It tells us to watch the ants and learn a lesson from them. Like the ants, we need to be wise and work hard.

Follow the maze.

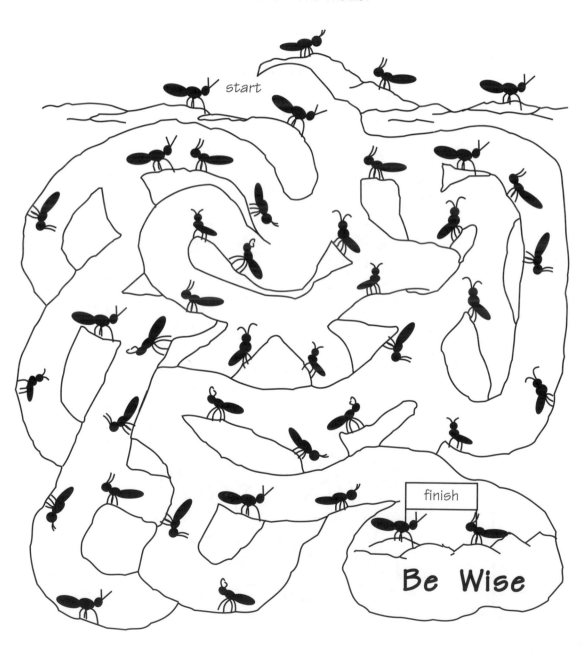

start

finish

Be Wise

# 47. Proverbs 17:17

Fill in the correct word.

A friend _____ at all times.

Proverbs 17:17

FRIENDS
ARE
SPECIAL!

The best F R I E N D

(Trace over the dotted lines)

to have is  __  __  __  __  __.

(Put the first letter of the pictures on the lines)

# 48. Ecclesiastes 3:1-8

Fill in the blanks matching the times to the words.

In verse 4 there is a time to _____ and a time to _____.
10:00                       4:00

In verse 8, it says a time to _____ before a time to hate.
12:00

Read verse 3 to find out that after a time to _____ is a
time to _____.                                          5:00
1:00

Verse 2 says there is a time to be _____, a time to _____, and
a time to _____.                8:00                    3:00
7:00

The last time mentioned in verse 4 is a time to _____.
9:00

In verse 6, the third time is a time to _____.
2:00

Verse 8 says not only is there a time for _____, but there
is also a time for _____.             11:00
6:00

# 49. Isaiah 1:18

1. Glue cotton balls on the areas marked.
2. Cut out snowflake and use a paper punch to make holes in the ends of the snowflake.
3. Hang up with string.

glue a cotton ball here

glue a cotton ball here

glue a cotton ball here

glue a cotton ball here

glue a cotton ball here

glue a cotton ball here

Your sins... shall be as white as snow.

Isaiah 1:18

# 50. Isaiah 26:3

Use words from Isaiah 26:3 to fill in the blanks.

P _ _ _ _ _ _

_ E _ P

PEACE

_ _ C _ _ _ _

_ H _ _ E

# 51. Isaiah 65:24

Use the letters on the telephone to match the code.

\_\_ E \_\_ O \_\_ E    \_\_ \_\_ E \_\_ \_\_
 1     3     7       9    4      #

\_\_ A \_\_ \_\_    I   \_\_ I \_\_ \_\_
 2     5    5        *     5    5

A \_\_ \_\_ \_\_ E \_\_ .   Isaiah 65:24
   6    8    *     7

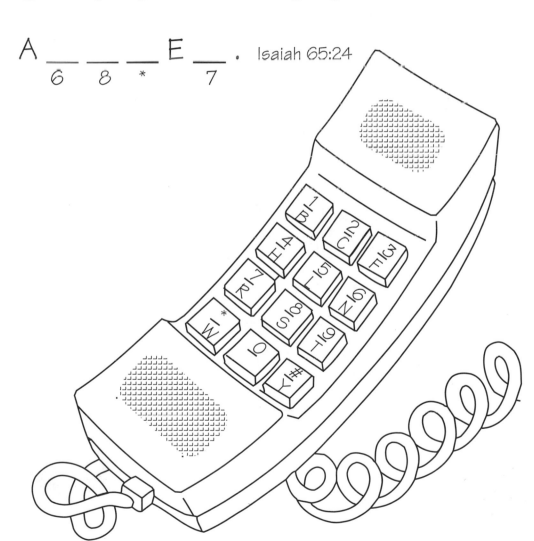

# 52. Jeremiah 17:9

Look up Jeremiah 17:9 in your Bible. Find all the words from the verse in the puzzle below.

```
O U I S        A N D A
K N O W A    E V E R L
C P D E S P E R A T E L Y
U L E H E D L P M E T P C
R E R A H E A R T E H L A
E A S W I C K E D E I T N
S T S B E Y O N D N E
E A G O I D P W L G A
  N S E T G O H D S
  D P L F A B O V E
    I O U E A S D
      L E G
        O
```

# 53. Books of the New Testament

Matthew
Mark
Luke
John
Acts
Romans
1 Corinthians
2 Corinthians
Galatians

Ephesians
Philippians
Colossians
1 Thessalonians
2 Thessalonians
1 Timothy
2 Timothy
Titus
Philemon

Hebrews
James
1 Peter
2 Peter
1 John
2 John
3 John
Jude
Revelation

Read each sentence below. Put the correct letter on the line to the right. Use these letters to fill in the blanks at the bottom of the page.

1.  What is the first letter of the fourth book? _____

2.  The second to the last letter in the first book is _____

3.  After John, the next eight books end with the letter _____

4.  Luke, Titus, and Jude all contain one letter alike. It is _____

5.  The book before Philemon ends with the letter _____

6.  The second letter in the book after Acts is _____

7.  In the third book, what is the second letter? _____

8.  The book after Jude starts with the letter _____

9.  Colossians has three of which letter? _____

10. The fifth book starts with the letter _____

11. The last book contains a letter no other book has. It is _____

12. Philippians has a vowel in it three times. It is _____

13. The book after Acts has in it S, N, M, R, A, and _____

14. What is the third letter in the book between Matthew and Luke? _____

**The New Testament is about**

__ __ __ __ __   __ __ __ __   __ __ __ __ __ __

# 54. Matthew 1:23

Read Matthew 1:23.

**What will the child be named?**

___ M M ___ N ___ ___ L

(Fill in the missing letters)

The child's name had a special meaning. Write the letter that is different in each column to find out the special meaning.

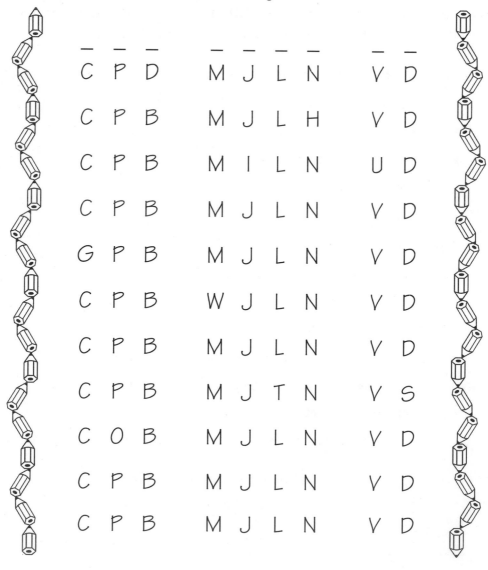

| C | P | D | | M | J | L | N | | V | D |
|---|---|---|---|---|---|---|---|---|---|---|
| C | P | B | | M | J | L | H | | V | D |
| C | P | B | | M | I | L | N | | U | D |
| C | P | B | | M | J | L | N | | V | D |
| G | P | B | | M | J | L | N | | V | D |
| C | P | B | | W | J | L | N | | V | D |
| C | P | B | | M | J | L | N | | V | D |
| C | P | B | | M | J | T | N | | V | S |
| C | O | B | | M | J | L | N | | V | D |
| C | P | B | | M | J | L | N | | V | D |
| C | P | B | | M | J | L | N | | V | D |

# 55. Matthew 4:19

Jesus said he would make us fishers of men if we follow him. How many fish are in the picture below? _____

Color the picture.

# 56. Matthew 5:1–12

## The Beatitudes

Find the following words in the puzzle at the bottom of this page. These words are from Matthew 5:1–12.

HEAVEN
REJOICE
GLAD
GREAT
PERSECUTE
KINGDOM
RIGHTEOUSNESS
REWARD
BEFORE
PURE
EARTH
PROPHETS
GOD
CALLED
PEACEMAKERS
HEART

MERCY
HUNGER
THIRST
MEEK
COMFORTED
MOURN
THEIRS
INHERIT

```
            G L A D A C D P
          P R O P H E T S O E
        T K M T D S U P H H R R
      C A B S H N P U R E T U I K E S
    O H P Q R B P E A C E M A K E R S J E
  M O U R N D E S I H G O H T I U S C O C
  E P N S A H F N R N R K S N N W T D I U
  R I G H T E O U S N E S S O G X A F C T
  C T E K B A R U S C A L L E D S Y G E E
  Y U R M C V E E A R T H P S O Z B H K J
  H E A R T E A R E W A R D T M E E K L I
  D A Y P I N H E R I T C O M F O R T E D
```

# 57. Matthew 5:16

Below are some words from Matthew 5:16. Print them in the puzzle in the correct spaces.

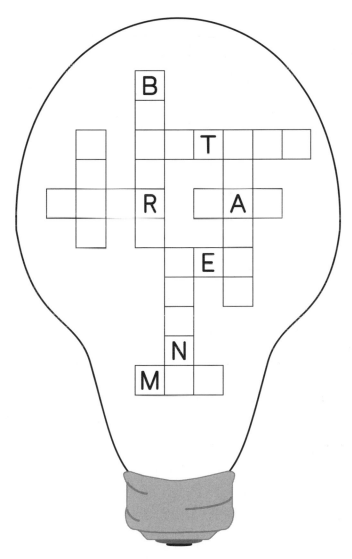

FATHER                    MAY                    HEAVEN

GOOD                      SEE                     MEN

YOUR                     BEFORE                  SHINE

# 58. Matthew 6:19–20

Read Matthew 6:19–20 and answer the questions by drawing a line to the correct picture.

What is one thing that could happen if our treasures are only on earth?

Where should our treasures not be?

Where should our treasures be?

# 59. Matthew 10:31

**Color by number.**

Jesus watches over and cares for the sparrow. Surely he will care for you.

1 = black       2 = brown       3 = green

# 60. Matthew 10:42

The following are some words from Matthew 10:42. Put them in the correct spaces in the puzzle.

COLD          LOSE          HIS
WATER         LITTLE        REWARD
TO            DISCIPLE      YOU
HE

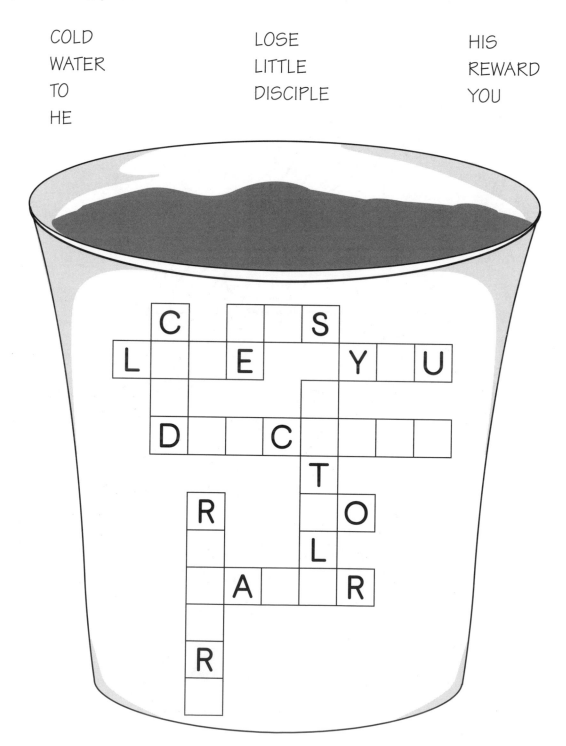

# 61. Matthew 11:28

Color the picture.

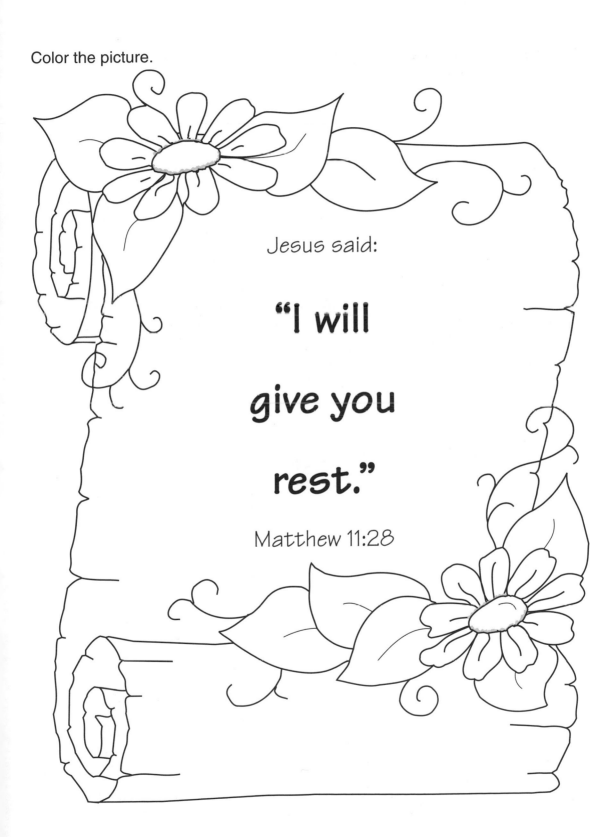

Jesus said:

"I will

give you

rest."

Matthew 11:28

# 62. Matthew 19:24

Start at the ★ and put the missing words on the lines below.

Jesus said:

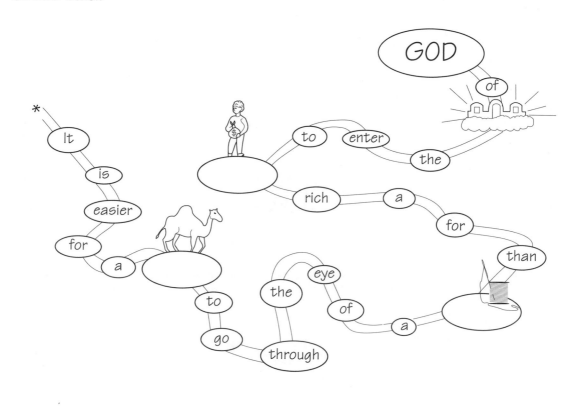

_____

_____

_____

_____

# 63. Matthew 22:37

Complete the sentence by filling in the blanks with the first letter of the picture below the line.

**We should love the Lord with all our**

\_\_\_\_\_ \_\_\_\_\_ \_\_\_\_\_ \_\_\_\_\_ \_\_\_\_\_

\_\_\_\_\_ \_\_\_\_\_ \_\_\_\_\_ \_\_\_\_\_

\_\_\_\_\_ \_\_\_\_\_ \_\_\_\_\_ \_\_\_\_\_

# 64. Matthew 26:41

Trace over the dotted lines.

# 65. Mark 13:31

Read Mark 13:31 in your Bible. Print the verse on the lines below. Use some of the words in the picture to help you. (There will be some words you will not use.)

Mark 13:31

# 66. Luke 1:37

The following are the Spanish words for Luke 1:37. Look up the same verse in your Bible and print it on the lines at the bottom of this page.

PORQUE PARA DIOS NO HAY IMPOSIBLE.

_____

_____

_____

# 67. Luke 2:1–12

## The Birth of Jesus

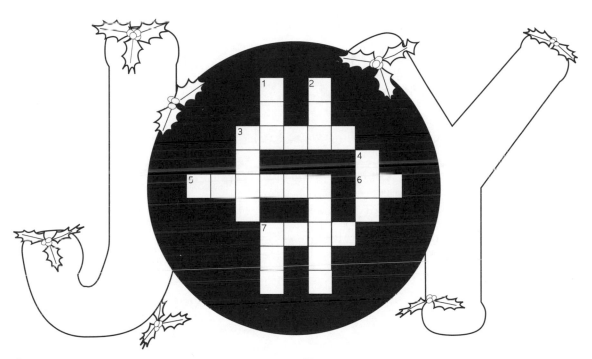

## Across

3. In verse 9 the shepherds saw an "_____ of the Lord."

5. "_____ also went up from . . . Nazareth" is in verse 4.

6. The word after "because" in verse 4 is _____

7. "And there _____ shepherds" is from verse 8.

## Down

1. "Room for them in the ____" is in verse 7.

2. "_____" were watching their flocks in verse 8.

3. The third word in verse 4 is _____.

4. "He is Christ ____ Lord" is in verse 11.

7. The fourth to the last word in verse 2 is ____ .

Cross out all the letters G, J, K, and X in the puzzle below. Put the remaining letters on the lines to find out why Mary laid baby Jesus in a manger.

```
X K B J E J C A U K S X
E G T H J K E X G R J E
W K X X A S J G N K O J
G K R O J X O M J X G K
F K O J X R K X G T H E
K M X G I J N J T K X G
H G J E K I X G K X N N
```

\_ \_ \_ \_ \_ \_ \_   \_ \_ \_ \_ \_   \_ \_ \_   \_ \_   \_ \_ \_ \_

\_ \_ \_ \_   \_ \_ \_ \_   \_ \_ \_   \_ \_   \_ \_ \_

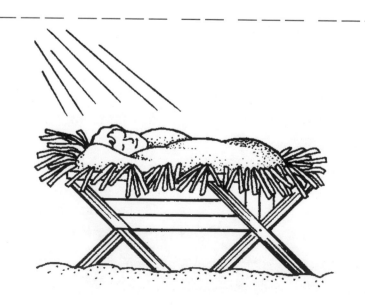

# 69. Luke 2:14a

Fill in the blanks using the code
in the small angels.

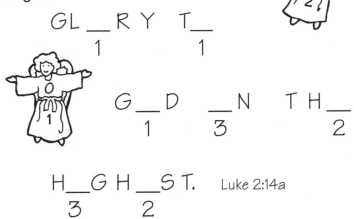

GL __ R Y T __
    1        1

G __ D __ N T H __
  1    3      2

H __ G H __ S T.   Luke 2:14a
 3    2

Make an angel.

1. Cut out on heavy line.
2. Apply glue to area A.
3. Overlap B to form a cone shape.

Example

of finished project

A

B

Glory to God
in the highest.

# 70. John 1:1

Solve the math problems under the lines. Match the answers to the same number of dots in the Bible cover at the bottom of this page. Put that word on the lines.

| _____ | _____ | _____ | _____ |
|--------|--------|--------|--------|
| 2+2 | 5-4 | 4+5-1 | 3+4 |
| 0+1 | 9-3 | 3+2 | 9-8 |
| 4+4-2 | 6+1 | 8-5 | 9-7 |
| 10-5 | 7-6 | 3+3 | 2+2+3 |

_____ .
9-7

# 71. John 11:25

1. Color the project below.
2. Cut out on outer lines.
3. Fold on dotted lines and set up as shown.

Example

of finished project

Fold on
dotted lines

Cut out on
outer lines.

I

am the

resurrection

and the

life.

John 11:25

# 72. John 14:1–6

Read this passage, then answer the following questions.

1. In verse 5, which
   disciple is mentioned?

\_\_ \_[1]\_ \_\_ \_\_ \_\_ \_\_

2. Jesus said he was
   going to prepare a

\_\_ \_\_ \_\_ \_\_ \_[2]\_

3. In verse 6, Jesus said:
   I am the

\_\_ \_[3]\_ \_\_

4. Not only is Jesus
   the way and the truth,
   but he is the

\_\_ \_\_ \_\_ \_[4]\_

5. Can anyone come to the
   Father without going through
   Jesus?

\_[5]\_ \_\_

(Use the letters in the boxes from above to fill in the spaces below.)

## JESUS IS THE ONLY WAY TO . . .

\_\_ \_\_ \_\_ ^V \_\_ \_\_
1  2  3    4  5

# 73. John 14:27

Color the picture.

**PEACE**

**I LEAVE WITH YOU.**

John 14:27

# 74. John 20:31

Fill in the blanks by putting the letter in the alphabet that comes just before the letter under the line.

_B_ _E_ _L_ _I_ _E_ _V_ _E_
 C   F   M   J   F   W   F

_T_ _H_ _A_ _T_   _J_ _E_ _S_ _U_ _S_
 U   I   B   U     K   F   T   V   T

_I_ _S_   _T_ _H_ _E_   _C_ _H_ _R_ _I_ _S_ _T_'
 J   T     U   I   F     D   I   S   J   T   U

_T_ _H_ _E_   _S_ _O_ _N_   _O_ _F_
 U   I   F     T   P   O     P   G

_G_ _O_ _D_.   John 20:31
 H   P   E

If you believe on the Lord Jesus Christ, you will have everlasting

_L_ _I_ _F_ _E_

(Unscramble the boxed letters from the above project to find the answer.)

# 75. Romans 3:23

Use your Bible to fill in the missing letters.

✝✝✝✝✝✝✝✝✝✝✝✝✝✝✝✝✝✝✝✝✝✝✝

F_ R  A_ _   H_ VE

S_ N_ _ _ _   _ N_

_ _ _ _   SHOR_

_ _   _ H_

_ L_ _ Y  O_

_ OD. Romans 3:23

✝✝✝✝✝✝✝✝✝✝✝✝✝✝✝✝✝✝✝✝✝✝✝

# 76. Romans 5:8

Trace over the dotted lines.

DIED FOR US.

**Cross Art Project**
1. Color and cut out on outer lines.
2. Fold back on dotted lines.
3. Stand up.

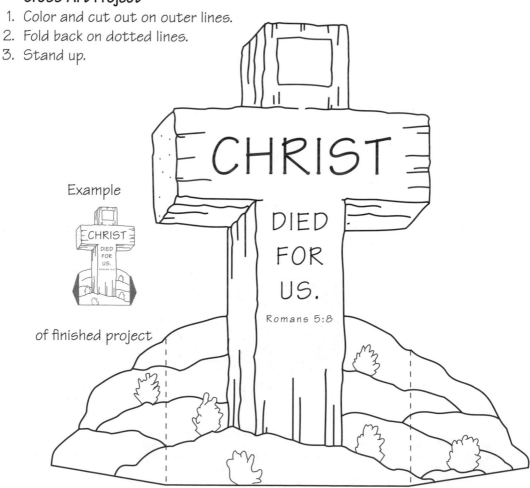

Example

of finished project

CHRIST

DIED
FOR
US.

Romans 5:8

# 77. Romans 10:9

Read the Bible passage. Then fill in the blanks using words from the word bank at the bottom of the page.

    According to Romans 10:9, you should _____ with your _____ the Lord Jesus.

    Also, you need to believe it in your _____ .

    When you _____ that God raised _____ from the dead, you will be _____ .

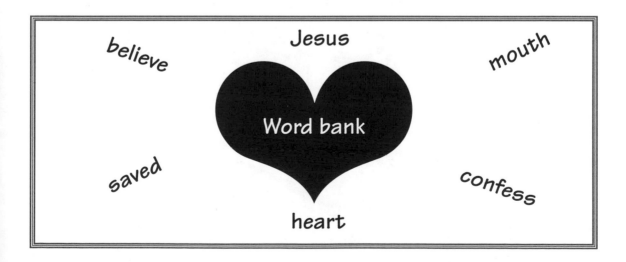

# 78. 1 Corinthians 14:1

Look up the passage in your Bible. Follow the words through the maze.

# 79. Ephesians 2:8–9

Use words from Ephesians 2:8–9 to fill in the blanks.

Aa  Bb  Cc  Dd  Ee  Ff  Gg  Hh  Ii  Jj  Kk  Ll  Mm

You are saved by _____
Rhymes with race

through _____ .
Unscramble these letters  T A H F I

You cannot be saved by y __ __ r s __ lf.
Fill in the spaces
with vowels

Since salvation is a _____
You receive this on your
birthday and special times

of God and not earned by your _____ ,
Third word in Ephesians 2:9

you cannot_____ about it.
Means proud

# 80. Ephesians 6:1

## Children, obey your parents!

Obey the following instructions to color the picture.

1. Color the letter after the "b" green.
2. Color the large "o" red.
3. Color the letter before the "e" blue.
4. Color the last letter in the word yellow.

**Children,
obey your parents in the
Lord, for this is right.**

Ephesians 6:1

# 81. Philippians 4:4

Color the picture.

REJOICE IN THE LORD.

Philippians 4:4

# 82. Philippians 4:11

Put the letter that is different in each column on the line at the top of that column.

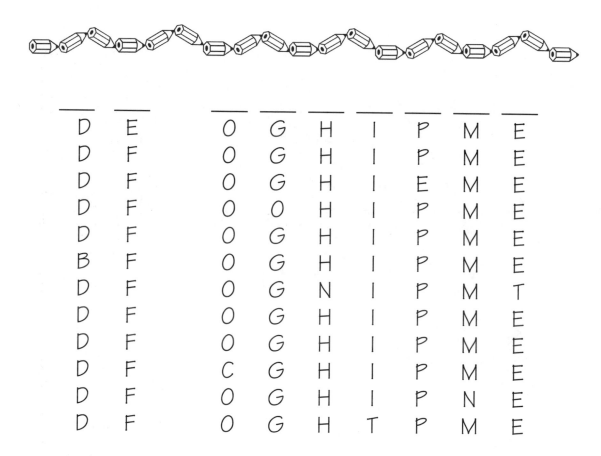

| D | E | O | G | H | I | P | M | E |
|---|---|---|---|---|---|---|---|---|
| D | E | O | G | H | I | P | M | E |
| D | F | O | G | H | I | P | M | E |
| D | F | O | G | H | I | E | M | E |
| D | F | O | O | H | I | P | M | E |
| D | F | O | G | H | I | P | M | E |
| B | F | O | G | H | I | P | M | E |
| D | F | O | G | N | I | P | M | T |
| D | F | O | G | H | I | P | M | E |
| D | F | O | G | H | I | P | M | E |
| D | F | C | G | H | I | P | M | E |
| D | F | O | G | H | I | P | N | E |
| D | F | O | G | H | T | P | M | E |

# 83. Philippians 4:13

Color in the dotted areas to find out who gives us strength.

# 84. Philippians 4:19

Look up Philippians 4:19 and circle all the words from the verse in the puzzle below.

```
I S U P P L M D O J
N A T L H A E L K E
B C O A L N E E D S
U C W N H A T T Q U
T O D D B S T H I S
U R I C H E S P C B
C D E F Y G H I H J
W I L L O G L O R Y
K N H M U Y Z W I S
A G L O R I O U S G
L B U S T P B S T O
L M Y M H I N T U D
```

# 85. 1 Thessalonians 5:18

Color the picture.

# 86. Hebrews 6:19

According to Hebrews 6:19, our hope in the Lord is like an _____ .

Color in the areas that have a dot in them to find the answer.

# 87. Hebrews 12:29

Do the dot-to-dot to find out what to write on the lines below.

FOR
OUR GOD
IS A
CONSUMING

_ _ _ _

# 88. Hebrews 13:8

Fill in the blanks using the code instructions at the bottom of the page.

## Jesus Christ is the same

$\underline{\phantom{x}}$ $\underline{\phantom{x}}$ $\underline{\phantom{x}}$ $\underline{\phantom{x}}$ $\underline{\phantom{x}}$ $\underline{\phantom{x}}$ $\underline{\phantom{x}}$ $\underline{\phantom{x}}$ $\underline{\phantom{x}}$

J   P   K   L   P   D   W   H   J

$\underline{\phantom{x}}$ $\underline{\phantom{x}}$ $\underline{\phantom{x}}$    $\underline{\phantom{x}}$ $\underline{\phantom{x}}$ $\underline{\phantom{x}}$ $\underline{\phantom{x}}$ $\underline{\phantom{x}}$

H   B   W    L   G   W   H   J

$\underline{\phantom{x}}$ $\underline{\phantom{x}}$ $\underline{\phantom{x}}$    $\underline{\phantom{x}}$ $\underline{\phantom{x}}$ $\underline{\phantom{x}}$ $\underline{\phantom{x}}$ $\underline{\phantom{x}}$ $\underline{\phantom{x}}$ $\underline{\phantom{x}}$.

H   B   W    C   G   D   P   E   P   D

Change any letter "H" to "A"

Change any letter "W" to "D"

Change any letter "G" to "O"

Change any letter "L" to "T"

Change any letter "D" to "R"

Change any letter "P" to "E"

Change any letter "C" to "F"

Change any letter "E" to "V"

Change any letter "J" to "Y"

Change any letter "K" to "S"

Change any letter "B" to "N"

# 89. James 4:7

Color by number using this code:

1 = YELLOW    2 = RED    3 = PURPLE    4 = BLUE

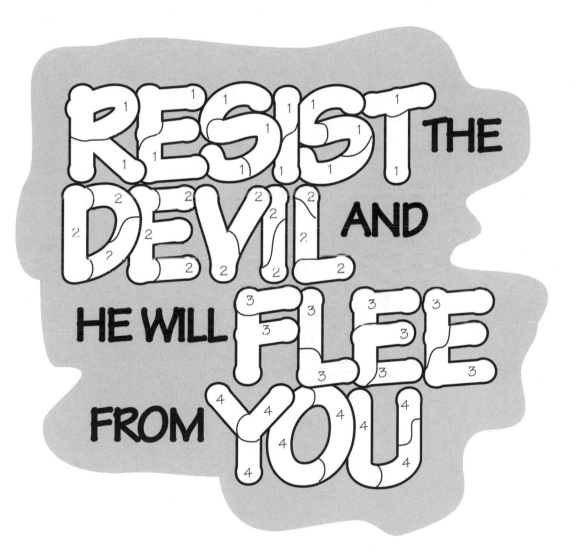

# 90. 1 John 4:7

Trace over the dotted lines.

Let us LOVE one another.

To make:
Color the dog and tail. Cut out. Insert a brass fastener in the small hole in the back of the dog and then in the hole in the tail. Make the dog wag its tail!

Let us love one another.

1 John 4:7

TAIL

# Answers

## 1. BOOKS OF THE OLD TESTAMENT

GENESIS, EXODUS, LEVITICUS, NUMBERS, DEUTERONOMY, JOSHUA, JUDGES, RUTH, 1 SAMUEL, 2 SAMUEL, 1 KINGS, 2 KINGS, 1 CHRONICLES, 2 CHRONICLES, EZRA, NEHEMIAH, ESTHER, JOB, PSALMS, PROVERBS, ECCLESIASTES, SONG OF SONGS, ISAIAH, JEREMIAH, LAMENTATIONS, EZEKIEL, DANIEL, HOSEA, JOEL, AMOS, OBADIAH, JONAH, MICAH, NAHUM, HABAKKUK, ZEPHANIAH, HAGGAI, ZECHARIAH, MALACHI

## 2. GENESIS 1:1

HEAVENS, EARTH

## 3. GENESIS 1:27

GOD CREATED MAN IN HIS OWN IMAGE.

## 4. GENESIS 2:7

## 5. GENESIS 18:14

## 6. EXODUS 20:12

FATHER, MOTHER

## 8. JOSHUA 1:8

1. LAW  2. MOUTH  3. MEDITATE  4. DAY, NIGHT
5. WRITTEN  6. PROSPEROUS

## 9. JOSHUA 23:11

LOVE THE LORD YOUR GOD.

## 10. JOSHUA 24:15

BUT AS FOR ME AND MY HOUSEHOLD, WE WILL SERVE THE LORD.

## 12. 1 SAMUEL 16:7

MAN LOOKS AT THE OUTWARD APPEARANCE, BUT THE LORD LOOKS AT THE HEART.

## 13. 2 CHRONICLES 20:15

FOR THE BATTLE IS NOT YOURS, BUT GOD'S.

## 14. JOB 29:3

1. RED  2. PURPLE  3. BLUE  4. WHITE  5. YELLOW
6. BLACK

## 15. PSALM 1

THE, OF, LAW, LORD, NIGHT, PLANTED, STAND, NOR, RIGHTEOUS, TREE

## 16. PSALM 2:11

SERVE THE LORD WITH FEAR AND REJOICE WITH TREMBLING.

## 17. PSALM 7:17

SING PRAISE TO THE NAME OF THE LORD.

## 18. PSALM 17:8

KEEP ME AS THE APPLE OF YOUR EYE; HIDE ME IN THE SHADOW OF YOUR WINGS.

## 20. PSALM 24:8

LORD

## 21. PSALM 25:4

SHOW ME YOUR WAYS, O LORD, TEACH ME YOUR PATHS.

## 24. PSALM 33:12

BLESSED IS THE NATION WHOSE GOD IS THE LORD.

## 25. PSALM 34:8

TASTE AND SEE THAT THE LORD IS GOOD.

## 26. PSALM 34:15

## 27. PSALM 37:1–8

1. FRET  2. LORD  3. ENVIOUS  4. GRASS
5. NOT  6. DELIGHT  7. GREEN  8. HEART
9. WAIT  10. COMMIT

## 29. PSALM 42:1

DEER, WATER, GOD

## 31. PSALM 46:10

BE STILL, AND KNOW THAT I AM GOD.

## 33. PSALM 51:2

CLEANSE ME FROM MY SIN.

## 34. PSALM 91:15

ANSWER, BE WITH, IN TROUBLE, DELIVER, AND HONOR

## 35. PSALM 100

LORD, GLADNESS, GOD, THANKSGIVING, LORD

## 37. PSALM 103:12

AS FAR AS THE EAST IS FROM THE WEST SO FAR HAS HE REMOVED OUR TRANSGRESSIONS FROM US.

## 38. PSALM 111:10

THE FEAR OF THE LORD IS THE BEGINNING OF WISDOM.

## 40. PSALM 118:24

THE LORD

## 43. PSALM 139:23

SEARCH ME, O GOD, AND KNOW MY HEART.

## 47. PROVERBS 17:17

LOVES, JESUS

## 48. ECCLESIASTES 3:1–8

WEEP, LAUGH, LOVE, KILL, HEAL, BORN, DIE, PLANT, DANCE, KEEP, WAR, PEACE

## 50. ISAIAH 26:3

PERFECT, KEEP, BECAUSE,

## 51. ISAIAH 65:24

BEFORE THEY CALL, I WILL ANSWER.

## 52. JEREMIAH 17:9

## 53. BOOKS OF THE NEW TESTAMENT

JESUS OUR SAVIOR

## 54. MATTHEW 1:23

IMMANUEL, GOD WITH US

## 56. MATTHEW 5:1–12

## 57. MATTHEW 5:16

### 60. MATTHEW 10:42

### 62. MATTHEW 19:24

CAMEL, NEEDLE, MAN, KINGDOM

### 63. MATTHEW 22:37

HEART, SOUL, MIND

### 65. MARK 13:31

HEAVEN AND EARTH WILL PASS AWAY, BUT MY WORDS WILL NEVER PASS AWAY.

### 66. LUKE 1:37

FOR NOTHING IS IMPOSSIBLE WITH GOD.

### 67. LUKE 2:1–12

### 68. LUKE 2:7

BECAUSE THERE WAS NO ROOM FOR THEM IN THE INN.

### 69. LUKE 2:14

GLORY TO GOD IN THE HIGHEST.

### 70. JOHN 1:1

IN THE BEGINNING WAS THE WORD, AND THE WORD WAS WITH GOD, AND THE WORD WAS GOD.

### 72. JOHN 14:1–6

THOMAS, PLACE, WAY, LIFE, NO

### 74. JOHN 20:31

BELIEVE THAT JESUS IS THE CHRIST, THE SON OF GOD.

### 75. ROMANS 3:23

FOR ALL HAVE SINNED AND FALL SHORT OF THE GLORY OF GOD.

### 77. ROMANS 10:9

CONFESS, MOUTH, HEART, BELIEVE, JESUS, SAVED

### 78. 1 CORINTHIANS 14:1

FOLLOW THE WAY OF LOVE.

### 79. EPHESIANS 2:8–9

GRACE, FAITH, YOURSELF, GIFT, WORKS, BOAST

### 82. PHILIPPIANS 4:11

BE CONTENT

### 84. PHILIPPIANS 4:19

### 87. HEBREWS 12:29

FIRE

### 88. HEBREWS 13:8

YESTERDAY AND TODAY AND FOREVER